DIANA

Children's Letters to God

HarperCollins*Publishers*

HarperCollins*Religious*
Part of HarperCollins*Publishers*
77-85 Fulham Palace Road, London w6 8jb

First published in Great Britain in 1997 by HarperCollins*Religious*
1 3 5 7 9 10 8 6 4 2

Copyright in this compilation © 1997 HarperCollins*Publishers* Ltd

The scripture quotation on p. 5 is taken from the New Revised
Standard Version of the Bible, © 1989 Division of Christian Education
of the National Council of Churches in the United States of America.

A catalogue record for this book
is available from the British Library

ISBN 0 551 03147 6

Printed and bound in Great Britain by
Bath Press ColourBooks, Glasgow

DIANA, PRINCESS OF WALES

1961-1997

It feels like a grief we shall never get over. The stunned disbelief at the death of Diana, Princess of Wales has reduced the world to tears and produced an outpouring of emotion never before witnessed in the twentieth century.

Those with faith, especially, have turned to God in their shock and sorrow to ask for His comfort, peace and courage. No prayers have been more poignant than those from children. Princess Diana had a special affection for, and way with, children, shown by her many letters, presents and visits to those who were ill or suffering. Many have since testified how her radiant smile and loving touch brought them joy and hope during their difficult times.

This is a beautiful collection of prayers by young children, all moved by their sadness to pray for good to come out of this most terrible tragedy. Their heartfelt prayers, simple yet powerful in the way only children's words can be, are presented here along with photographs of the People's Princess in her many roles – mother, helper, carer, campaigner, friend.

Love is patient; love is kind; love is not envious or boastful
or arrogant or rude. It does not insist on its own way; it is
not irritable or resentful; it does not rejoice in wrongdoing,
but rejoices in the truth. It bears all things, believes all
things, hopes all things, endures all things.

1 CORINTHIANS 13:4-7, NRSV

Dear Lord Jesus,
Thankyou Lord for bringing
a loving, kind and generous person
like Diana on Earth. She was
perfect in every way possible.
She's still perfect even though she's
gone but she's still alive in our
hearts
                    Amen
                        Natalie
                          Holmes
                            Age 10.

Arriving at the Field Museum in Chicago for a fund-raising dinner, 1996

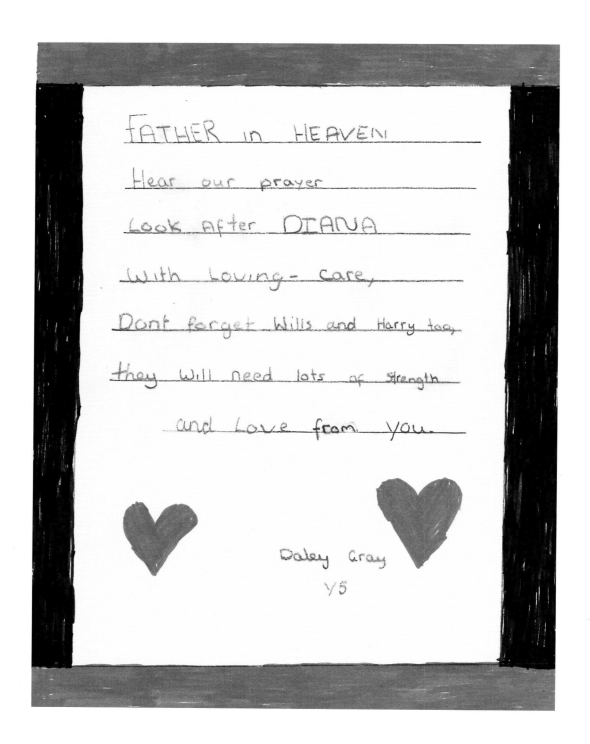

FATHER in HEAVEN

Hear our prayer

Look after DIANA

With Loving - Care,

Dont forget Wills and Harry too,

they will need lots of strength

and Love from you.

Daley Gray

Y5

With Mother Teresa, 1997

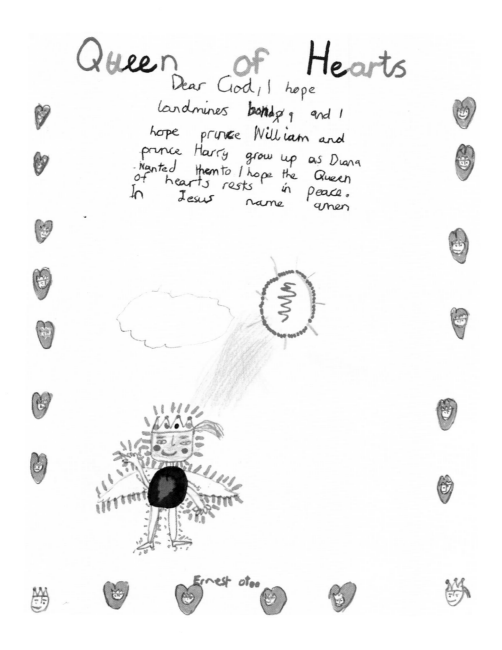

Queen of Hearts

Dear God, I hope landmines band, and I hope prince William and prince Harry grow up as Diana wanted them to I hope the Queen of hearts rests in peace. In Jesus name amen

Ernest otoo

During a visit to Leicester, 1997

Dear God,
I hope Diana is Happy in heaven and can you help Prince William and Prince harry to get over it it soon. I know thay are in a lot of Pain. So Please could you do it for me we will never forget her love and her caring ways

Amem

After the birth of Prince Harry, 1984

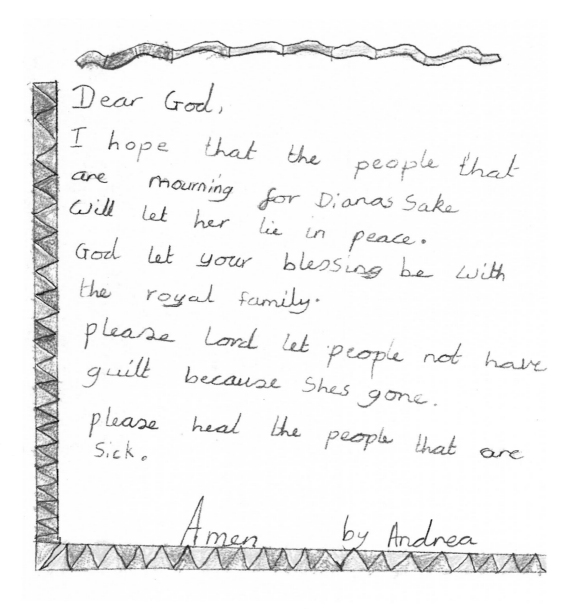

Dear God,

I hope that the people that are mourning for Dianas Sake will let her lie in peace.

God let your blessing be with the royal family.

please Lord let people not have guilt because Shes gone.

please heal the people that are Sick.

Amen   by Andrea

At Kensington Palace, celebrating the start of a fund-raising wheelchair push for the International Spinal Research Trust of which she was patron, 1996

Dear Lord,
        Please help princes
william and Harry
and all the royal family
to cope with the
loss of the princess.
The princess was
kind and she did
things things that
other peopil would
never do and we hope
that she is up in
heaven with you Amen.
name Ryan Dalgarno Age 9

With a young Prince Harry, 1987

16

Dear god
thank you for
Diana and thank you
for all the good
things she has
done.
Amen

courtnay
age 6

Shaking hands with singer David Bowie backstage at Wembley Arena
before the 1993 Concert of Hope

Gr

Grace (4 1/2)
"I liked her,
she was a
beautiful lady"

At the Council of Fashion Designers of America Awards, 1995

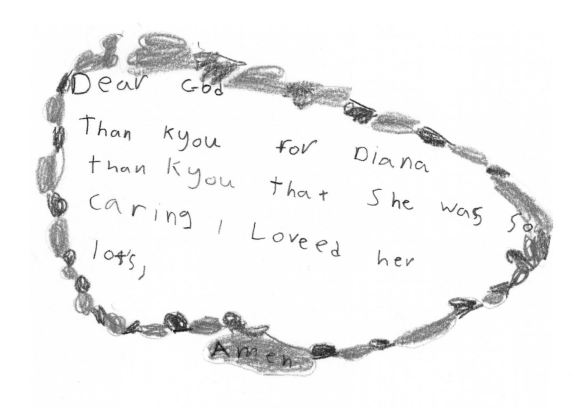

Dear God

Thankyou for Diana
thankyou that She was so
Caring I Loveed her
lots,

Amen

GraceL-b an 6

At the Tongogara refugee camp, Zimbabwe, 1993

Dear God, I know no one could replace Diana but please make us be kind in her ways she loved everyone. She helped the homeles, Cared for people with leprosy and wasn't afraid to touch people with aids Now she's gone were all sad.

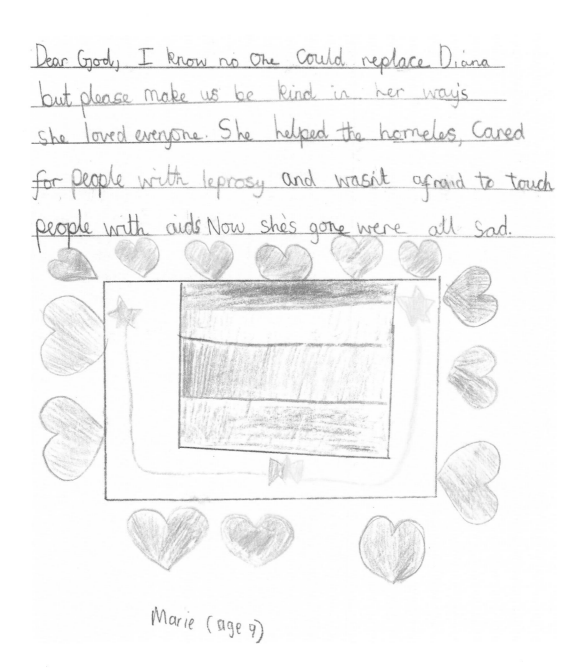

Marie (age 9)

During her visit to a health centre in the Angolan capital Luanda
to see the work of the British Red Cross, 1997

Dear Lord,
   Help us in this dark time. Help us through Dianas death, she was a kind and loving person, with a lot of care. Please look after her family keep them safe and care for them. Protect them from all harm.
   Amen.

   By Elizabeth Laws
        Beatham

   Age 10.

Visiting an old people's home in Taunton, Devon, 1992

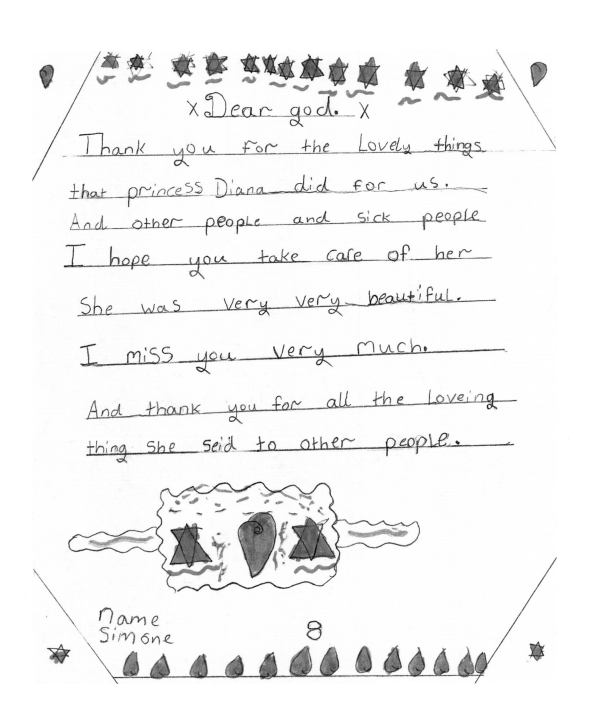

x Dear god. x

Thank you for the Lovely things
that princess Diana did for us.
And other people and sick people
I hope you take care of her
She was very very beautiful.

I miss you very much.

And thank you for all the loveing
thing she seid to other people.

Name
Simone   8

At Christie's before the sale of her dresses, 1997

Dear God

thank you that Diana
helped to stop land-
mines. Help prince
William and prince
Harry. and thankyou
that she was such a
nice lady Amen

wesley wroe Age 6

Diana with the rose named after her in aid of lung disease research, 1997

Dear Lord Jesus

I am so sorry that Diana is dead but she is in the best and the safest place she can ever be and it was a shock to the whole world

Amen

by Andy Constantinou Age 10

At the Taj Mahal, 1992

Dear God

We know Princess Diana was always kind

She helped the sick the needy and the blind

We felt her love we shared her pain

She'll always be that special link in the chain

That joins our hearts and your love

Diana will always be the brightest star in the sky

Alexandria Hilden-Hall

Age 10   Y6

St. Mary Magdalene

Hollway London

In Lahore, 1997

Dear God,

thank you for a lovly princess called Diana. She was the queen of our hearts and she will still be our queen of heart. We will never forget you, our mind and our heart will always think of you. I'm so sad you died. When we go to heavan will meet you there, I hope you get arewerd in heaven, because you have done so much. We will never forget you of loving queen Diana. And our angel of light.

Amen

by faith williams
Age: 10

Visiting a Sydney hospital, 1996

Dear god

I houp Landmins
Stoq. amen.//

Ben.Hinson.Raven. age 6.

Talking to a volleyball team made up of victims of land-mines in Zenica, Bosnia, 1997

Dear god

Thank you for the time you let Diana
Help the Sick and Poor. And for mating
People happy Please can you make

her happy now She Is In heaven with
You. When you helped the poor
You were happy

Aman

Jack
Age 7

With Nicky Welsh, who was awaiting a lung transplant at the Brompton Hospital, 1997

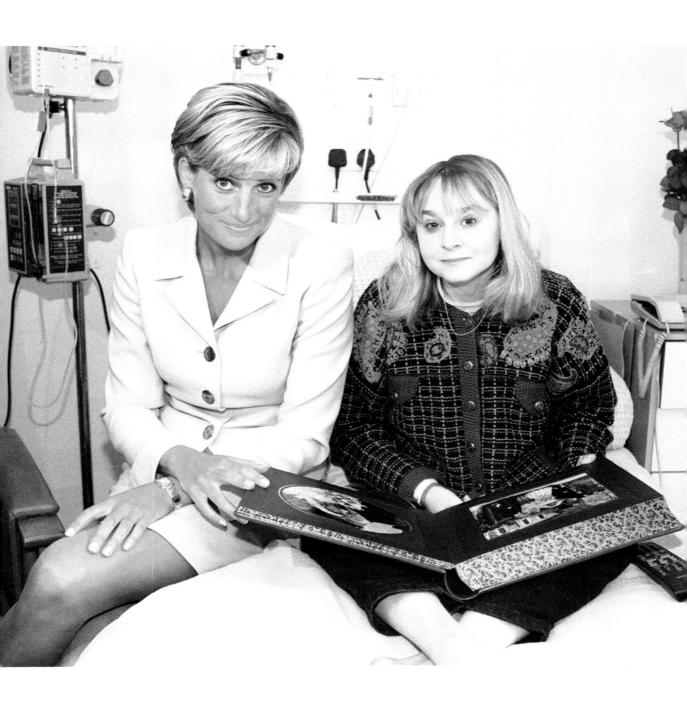

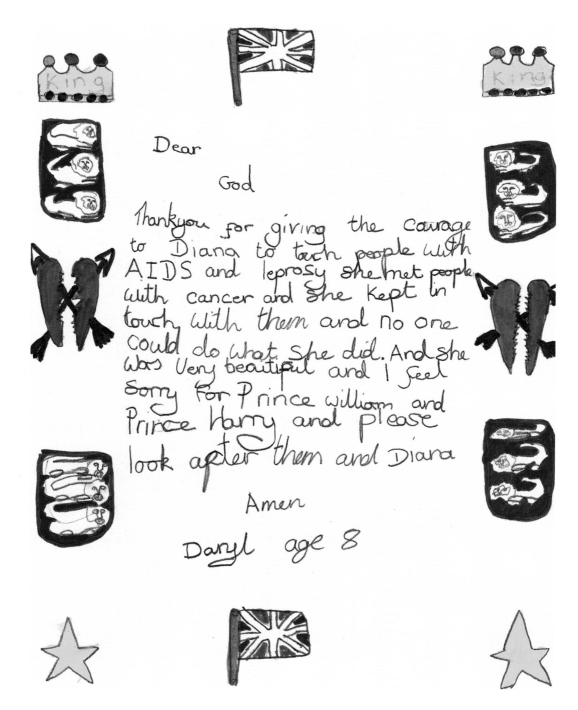

Dear

God

Thankyou for giving the courage to Diana to touch people with AIDS and leprosy she met people with cancer and she kept in touch with them and no one could do what she did. And she was very beautiful and I feel sorry for Prince William and Prince Harry and please look after them and Diana

Amen

Daryl age 8

At the New York Hilton, where she was honoured with a humanitarian award from the United Cerebral Palsy Society, 1995

Dear God,

Diana was a lovely person who liked to help as much as she could. Everybody who saw her when they were ill said that she looked like an angle up from heavan I hope now she has find peace at last.

Amen

by natasha Callis age 10

A loving word to a bridesmaid before her wedding to Prince Charles, 1981

Connor

Connor (4)

" Please look after the
Queen of the hearts
in heaven !"

The photocall after the wedding, 1981

Dear Lord Jesus

Diana the princess of Wales was a very nice woman
Please look after her and keep her safe in your care.
Also look after Prince William and Harry who are very
upset at the moment.
Dear Lord Jesus I would like you to help Prince Charles
to look after his children and let them go on all the
trips they used to with their mother.
On Prince Harrys birthday I hope he has a very nice
time and he isn't too sad Amen.

Leanna Ollivierre
Age 10

On the royal yacht Britannia, 1991

Dear God,
Thank you for all The
Loving Things princess-Diana
has done for us. Thank you for all
The sick people she had helped
and all The people with out two
Legs. Amen

From
Aaron Reid
X

With land-mine victims in Angola, 1997

Almighty God let us pray for prince Harry and prince william and charles in the future. Help those who princes Diana helped and carerd for. Make those who are scared to touch those with AiDS or any other kind of diseases make thos touch the people with diseases so they can feel that they are human not monsters. Diana was brave and caring so make those people the same as Diana. Amen

By Alisha Kasen zixxx

With an AIDS patient, 1991

52

David (4)

" My dear God
look after the Princess."

At the Dior party, 1996

Dear Lord Jesus, Diana was a Lovely
Person who We all loved dearly.
You Loaned her to us as a bud who
bloomed into a beautiful rose and
and the time has come for her to return
to your beautiful garden.
it is a shame that she had to leave
us because she was loved by everyone.
The greatest shame of all is that she
had to leave behind two loving sons
who will Miss her and the love she had
to give.
She had a big heart with enough love
to spread the whole world round.
Diana was the queen of all our hearts
especially of her family who will feel
her loss most of all.
Thank you for her time on earth.

A Men

Anthony Eamea age 10

At the North London Hindu temple, 1997

On a walkabout in Leeds, 1993

A prayer for Princess Diana

Dear god Diana was a very nice lady, she was not scared of people with disease, she helped other people that couldn't do things that we can.

Please help people that have been hurt by landmines to get better and please help Prince Harry and Prince William to be happier.

Armen.

By Frankie Allen. Age 8

Meeting children in Sarajevo during a two-day visit to Bosnia, 1997

Diana princess of
wales

by Darius Lester   Age: 10

William's school sports day, 1989

Dear God thanYou fo the Royal family and thanYou fo
Diana.
DAN 6

Dancing with Prince Charles in Australia, 1985

AMighty God, our Farther in hevean,

We Pray that you look aler Diana
because once She was one and a
million and I Pray For William and
Harry because they were very brave
at the Funeral and I Prax For her
and her Family and I think She
was very generous.

Amen.

BY Amiyna age :8

Preparing for a cycling trip, 1989

66

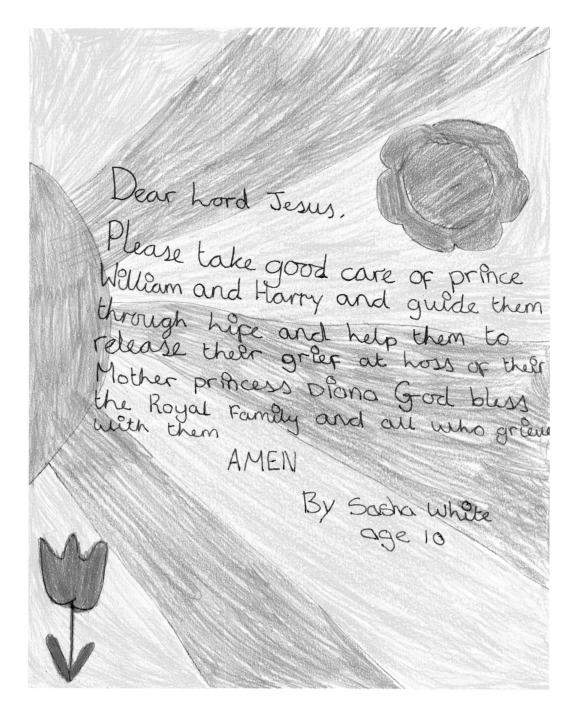

Dear Lord Jesus,

Please take good care of prince William and Harry and guide them through life and help them to release their grief at loss of their Mother princess Diana God bless the Royal Family and all who grieve with them

AMEN

By Sasha White age 10

Prince William goes home, 1982

8997

Dear God Tankyou for Diana
and all the love she gave
from her heart. Pleas Look
after a new angle in heaven.
Amen

Charles and Diana with the Pope at the Vatican, 1985

Diana is our Princess

Dear god

Diana was a lovely person in
every way. She touched people's hearts,
and now you have taken her from us.
I'm very sad, but I know that Diana
will be safe with you. in heaven

Amen
by Kelsey callis
age 7

Visiting the Brompton Hospital, 1997

Diana

Dear God,
          PLease look after princess Diana Well. because Diana is like a big sister and now she is gone.
It is a big Shock to every-one that princess Diana has died.
And I feel really Sorry for william and Harry. because they have no mum, but they only have their dad, grandma and granddad.
Well good-bye Diana.
          Amen.

your girl gone

we love you

Name
Re Mel

Age
8

An official family portrait from 1984

Dear Lord,

Look after our dear princess,
who's death was very tragic,
Who Supported many charitys,
and whatever She did Seemed magic.

She talked to landmine victims,
and people with Lepracy too,
She didn't Seem Scared of anything,
and she loved both the people and you.

As the coffin went by all was Silent,
for miles from here to there,
The Queen of hearts is now all yours,
the sweetest angel in your care.

She was not born a princess,
but earned a place in our hearts,
Please cherish and embrace our Diana,
the Queen of everyones heart
            Amen

        Fabia cooper
                    Age 10

Inspecting the troops of the Second Battalion of the Princess of Wales' Royal
Regiment at the presentation of colours at Howe Barracks, Kent, 1995

Dear God please help people
keep up the good work diana
started and I thank you
God for the kindness Diana
Showed For the poor and

the needy and I thank
you God for helping Diand
Stop land mines.
Amen.
by Nathan
age 8.

With Sandra Tigica, 13 (left) at the orthopaedic workshop near Luanda, 1997

Dear Lord Jesus

You are the fountain of all
hope and goodness. Help us to
remember Diana in as many ways
as we can. The queen of hearts
is gone but our Holy father is here
with us.   Amen.

BY Nichola Ward
age 10

Arriving at the Sydney Entertainment Centre, 1996

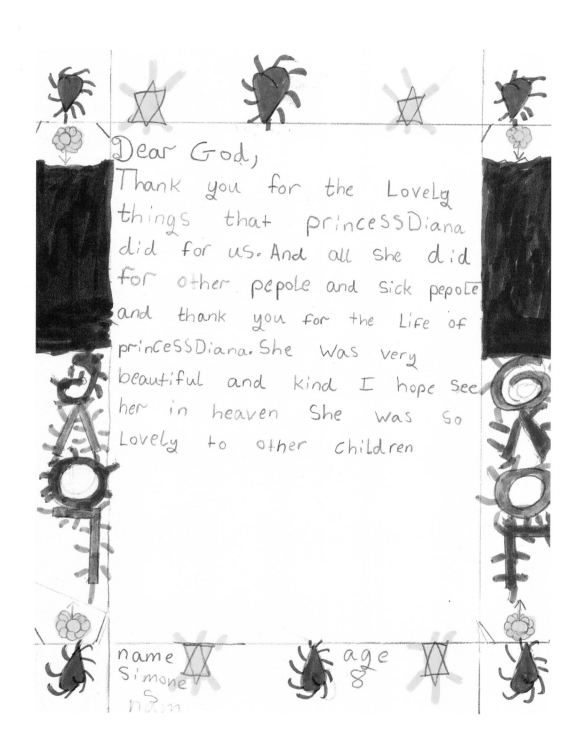

Dear God,
Thank you for the Lovely
things that princess Diana
did for us. And all she did
for other pepole and sick pepole
and thank you for the Life of
princess Diana. She was very
beautiful and kind I hope see
her in heaven She was so
Lovely to other children

name
Simone
naim

age
8

Meeting Holly Ann Robinson Marsh at Northwick Park Hospital, near Harrow, 1997

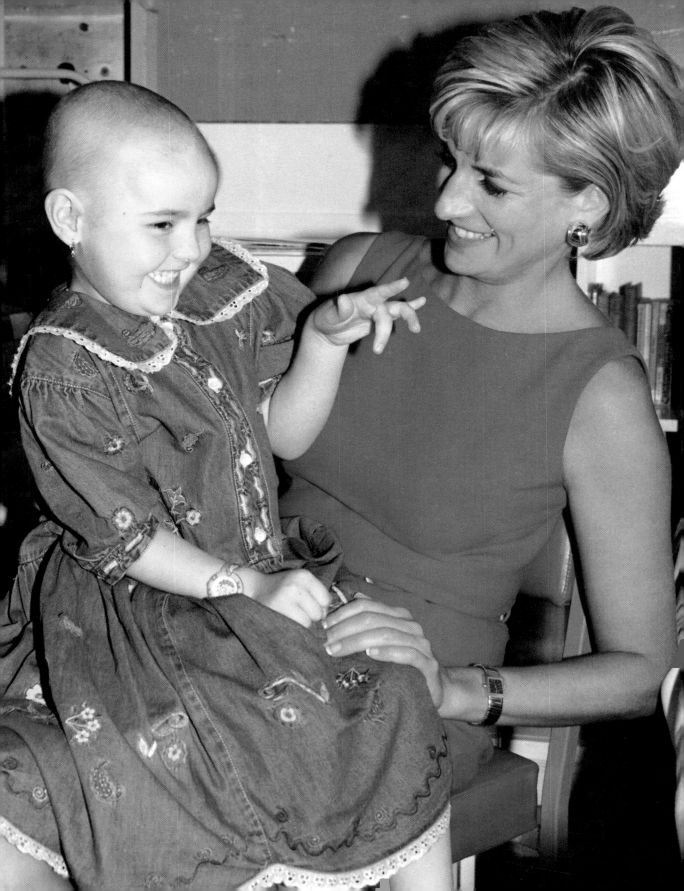

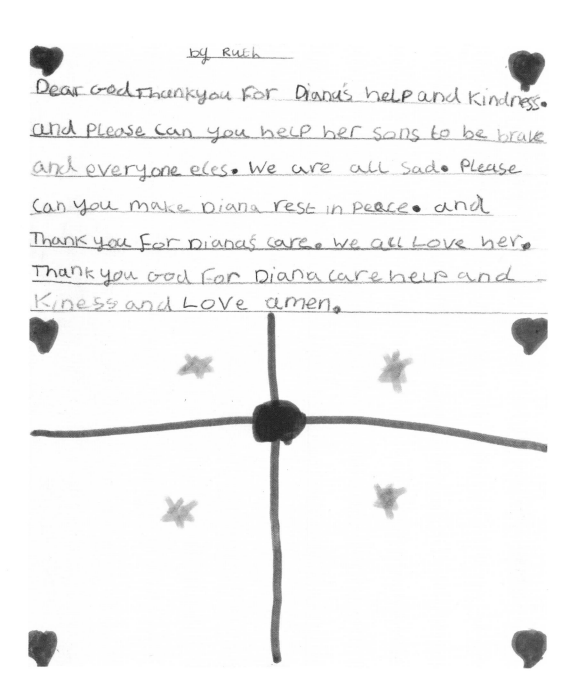

by Ruth

Dear God Thankyou for Diana's help and kindness. and Please can you help her sons to be brave and everyone eles. We are all sad. Please can you make Diana rest in peace. and Thank you for Dianas care. we all Love her. Thank you God for Diana care help and Kiness and Love amen.

Talking to building workers during a walkabout in Oxford, 1993

84

Dear ♥ God, ✦

I thank you for Princess
di. For ✦ and she
thused Pelpel 🙂 whev
laprse and whev ✦
Sansa But nau she ○
is 🙂 gon and we ✦
love her ♥ even more
✦ ✦ Amen age...8

At the child feeding scheme at Nemazuva school, during her visit to Zimbabwe, 1993

Dear Lord, Please help the princes and the queen and the roytal family and William and Harry and make them feu happy because now they are sad. Amen Age8 Andrew c

Watching the Trooping of the Colour, 1992

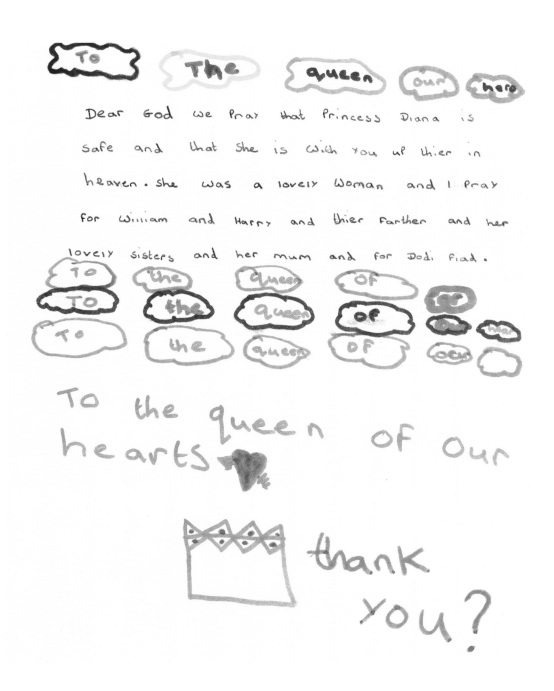

To The queen our hero

Dear God we Pray that Princess Diana is safe and that she is with you up thier in heaven. she was a lovely woman and I Pray for William and Harry and thier Farther and her lovely sisters and her mum and for Jodi Fiad.

To the queen of
To the queen of
To the queen of

To the queen of our hearts

thank you?

Diana and her mother, Frances Shand Kydd, at her brother Charles' wedding, 1989

Dear

Dear God

Thank you for bringing up Diana she was
really good to us she help little babys that
was really ill. She helped people with aids
she helped ~~disabled~~ disabled people
She was really kind to us.

Amen

At the British Paraplegic Sports Society Ball, 1989

Dear God

PLease Look after prince

WiLLiam and Prince Harry
and Look after princess
Diana in Heaven

Amen

Love from

WiLLiam
Sharp   age 5

At Thorpe Park amusement park, 1992

Dear God thank you

for Diana Princess of Wales
Queen of Heart We Shall
miss you. I only hope Someone
Can continue your good
Work may you rest in peace

Good bless William, Harry
and Prince Charles.

by ope age 7

With her family, 1991

Dear Lord Jesus,

Diana helped us all,
She helped the sick &
poor. She was kind to
those in need. Please
be kind to the Princes,
William and Harry, like
Diana was kind to us.
Stay with them for ever
and look af ter them,

A men

Elizabeth Laws
Beatham

age 10.

At Great Ormond Street Hospital, 1997

Dear God,

Thank you for Princess Diana and all the work she did. Thank you for the courage and bravery that she showed. By touching people with leprosy and AIDS she made people less afraid of these illnesses. please help us to respect and treat sick people normally. please help us to follow Princess Diana's example and please bless people who are carrying on her work.

Amen

Michaela Hinson-Raven
Age 8

At an old age welfare centre in Hyderabad, 1992

Dear God Please look after princess Diana Prince William and Prince Harry Please look after the people Princess Diana Looked after I hope that they live longer and I hope everyone will cheer up soon and so do the two prince's and Prince Wales.

A. men

by Kaya 8 years old

Skiing in Lech, Austria, 1991

Dear God

Please will you be with everyone now because we have a big hole in our hearts, the hole that Diana Filled up. I'm missing her already.

By Stacy Ramsey.

(aged – 9½)

Dinner at the New York Hilton where she received her humanitarian award from the United Cerebral Palsy Society, 1995

Dear God, Diana was a great women and she did alot of things to help people like Land Mines and aids, cancer and children that were sick. Thank-you for princess Diana but why did you take her away so soon. I'll always have a place in my heart for princess Diana, Queen of heart's

We Miss princess Diana.

Amen.

By: Bianca Marquez age: 9

In memory of princess Diana

An AIDS conference, 1991

106

NATIONAL AIDS TRUST

Children
and AIDS

NATIONAL CHILDREN'S BUREAU

Dear God,

                 I just pray for the royal family and the tow princes who have lost their mum forever and I feel very sorry for prince Harry and prince william because they have not just lost their mum but they have lost the most beautyful wonderful, and a caring lady I have ever heard of and please look after william and Harry.

                    A men

chelsea 9

Prince William's confirmation day, 1997

108

Visiting a day centre in Somerset, 1991

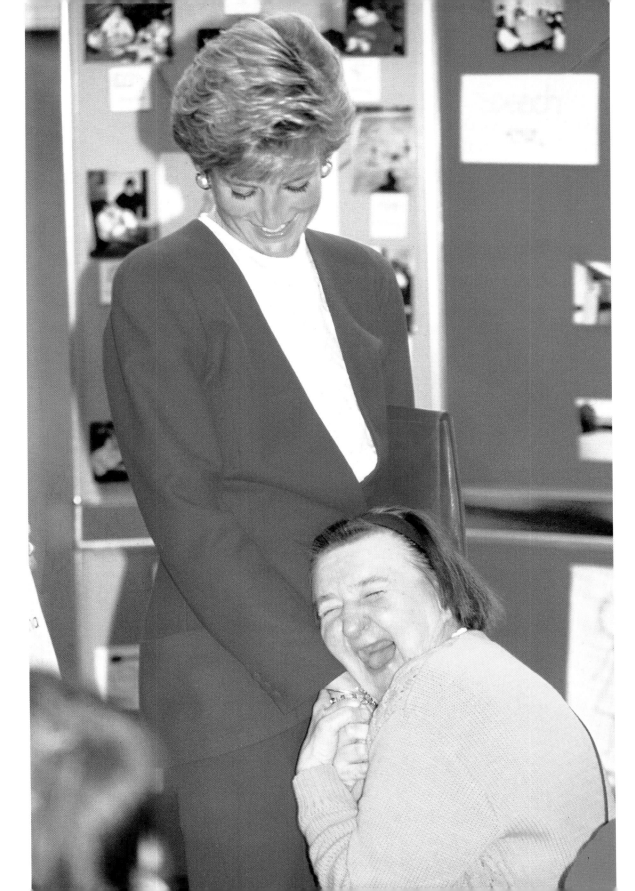

Tianna. age-7
Marquez

Dear gal:

Thank you for making
Princess diana and she
was a really kind and she
helped peoule wiht leprosey
and she try to stop Landmines
and she got taken away
from us she willalways queen
of are heats.

In Angola, 1997

112

At Northwick Park and St Mark's Hospital, 1997

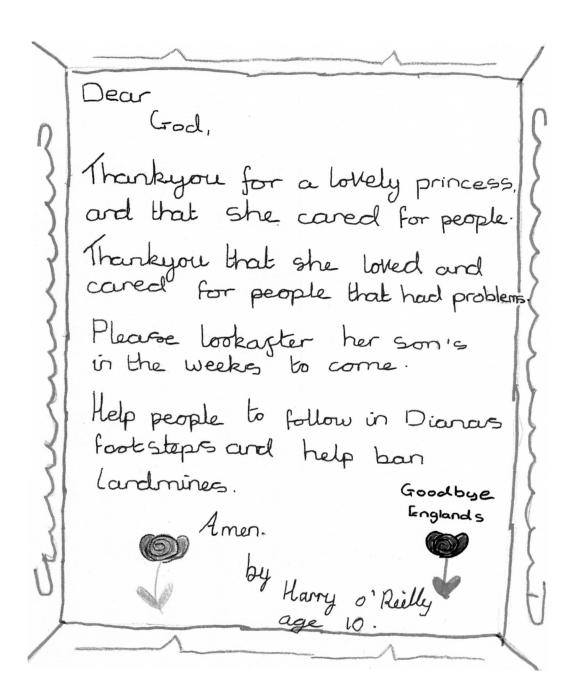

Dear
    God,

Thankyou for a lovely princess,
and that she cared for people.

Thankyou that she loved and
cared for people that had problems.

Please lookafter her son's
in the weeks to come.

Help people to follow in Dianas
footsteps and help ban
landmines.

                    Goodbye
                    Englands

        Amen.

        by Harry o'Reilly
        age 10.

In Angola, 1997

Dear God

I am sorry that this happened to Diana. This should not have happened because she is our Princess, and lots of People love her. Lots of People gave her flowers, poems, letters, balloons, and lots of things. We pray to you God at dinner, lunch, and breakfast. I hope Diana enjoys herself in heaven and I know you will look after her because you look after People who go to heaven. Lots and lots of People love Diana, the whole world, even I Love Diana. God, make sure she makes friends in heaven.

From Tamaszina Jacobs-Abiola
(7 years old - Islington, N1)

Diana, have a nice time in heaven.

Amen.

Diana

With Virginia Wade and Sir Cliff Richard at the opening ceremony
of the 1991 Federation Cup

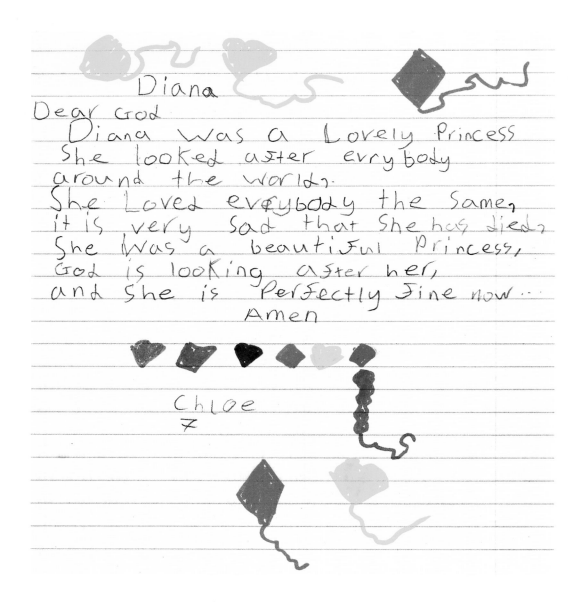

Diana

Dear God
  Diana was a Lovely Princess
She looked after evrybody
around the world.
She Loved everybody the Same,
it is very Sad that She has died,
She was a beautiful Princess,
God is looking after her,
and she is Perfectly fine now...
        Amen

Chloe
7

With actor Sylvester Stallone at the Champion Children Awards, 1993

To the most Fabulous God.

I hope you are taking care of Prince William and Prince Harry, aswell as Princess Diana and Dodi. I hope Princess Diana's death has not brought too much sadness to the Royal Family. Incleding Prince Charles, and Princess Diana's Family. I am sure Diana and Dodi will live in peace now, and will watch over Prince William and Prince Harry, and help them not to be too sad for very long. but most of all I hope you're taking care of everyone.

Armen.

By Tyler H-H.

Prince Harry joins Prince William for his first day at Wetherby School, 1989

Dear God
Please will you look after
Princess Diana for us
because we love her and miss
her Robert 6

The English National Ballet at the Royal Albert Hall, 1997

With particular thanks to Simon Marsh and the pupils of St Mary Magdalene Primary School, Holloway.

CREDITS